Contents

Any words appearing in bold, **like this**, are explained in the Glossary.

Was your pet once wild?

You may think that you just have a pet mouse or rat, but the mice and rats people keep as pets are very close to their wild relatives. Finding out more about the wild side of your pet will help you give it a better life.

There are many different types of mice and rats. If you are lucky, you may see wild mice or rats in your garden, around cities, and in the country.

Family

Did you know that rats and mice are related to lemmings, gerbils, and hamsters? They are all small **rodents**.

Wild rats like eating stored grain.

www.raintreepublishers.co.uk
Visit our website to find out more information about **Raintree** books.

To order:
☎ Phone 44 (0) 1865 888112
🖹 Send a fax to 44 (0) 1865 314091
🖥 Visit the Raintree Bookshop at **www.raintreepublishers.co.uk** to browse our catalogue and order online.

First published in Great Britain by Raintree, Halley Court, Jordan Hill, Oxford OX2 8EJ, part of Harcourt Education.
Raintree is a registered trademark of Harcourt Education Ltd.

Editorial: Melanie Copland and Sarah Chappelow
Design: Richard Parker and Tinstar Design Ltd (www.tinstar.co.uk)
Illustrations: Jeff Edwards
Picture Research: Mica Brancic and Charlotte Lippmann
Production: Duncan Gilbert

Originated by Ambassador Litho Ltd
Printed and bound in China by South China Printing Company

10 digit ISBN 1 8444 3930 5 (hardback)
13 digit ISBN 978 1 8444 3930 0 (hardback)
09 08 07 06 05
10 9 8 7 6 5 4 3 2 1

10 digit ISBN 1 8444 3936 4 (paperback)
13 digit ISBN 978 1 8444 3936 2 (paperback)
10 09 08 07 06
10 9 8 7 6 5 4 3 2 1

British Library Cataloguing in Publication Data
Waters, Jo
The Wild Side of Pet Mice & Rats
636.9352
A full catalogue record for this book is available from the British Library.

Acknowledgements
The publishers would like to thank the following for permission to reproduce photographs: Ardea p. **6** (Gary R. Jones), **21** (John Daniels); Bruce Coleman p. **22** (Jane Burton); FLPA pp. **7** (Silvestris Photoservice) **14**, **15**, **23**, **28**; Harcourt Education Ltd/Tudor Photography p. **5** (Gareth Boden) **13** (Gareth Boden) **17**, **19** (Gareth Boden); NHPA pp. **4** (Stephen Dalton), **8** (T. Kitchin & V. Hurst), **10** (Stephen Dalton), **16** (Eric Soder), **20** (Laurie Campbell), **24** (Mike Lane), **25** (ANT Photo Library), **26** (Daniel Heuclin), **27** (Stephen Dalton); RSPCA Photolibrary p. **9** (Angela Hampton); Science Photo Library p. **5**.

Cover photograph of a white mouse with bedding reproduced with permission of Corbis. Inset photograph of a harvest mouse on wheat reproduced with permission of Corbis (George McCarthy).

The publishers would like to thank Michaela Miller for her assistance in the preparation of this book.

Wild mice and rats have always lived near to people. They feed off our scraps and rubbish. They sleep and nest in our homes. They have even lived on ships at sea!

Rats and mice are intelligent and nosy creatures. They love to explore and play and they are interesting pets. They are also small, so they are good pets if you do not have much room.

Pet rats (bottom) are related to wild brown rats (top).

Types of mouse and rat

There are hundreds of different **species** of wild rat. Common ones are brown rats and black rats. There are also rats that look different from normal brown rats, such as the wood rat.

There are lots of different types of mouse. Some mice you can find in the wild are field mice, house mice, dormice, harvest mice, yellow necked mice, and spiny mice.

This grey bushytailed wood rat looks a bit like a squirrel.

There are many different types of pet mice. They are not all brown like wild mice. Pet mice come in many colours including white or **albino**, multi-coloured, and black.

The pet rat is related to the wild brown rat. Wild brown rats are always brown, but fancy rats also come in many colours including white, lilac, black, yellow, or with patches of different colours.

Pet mice and rats are similar to their wild relatives, but they are **domesticated**.

Where are mice and rats from?

Mice and rats live all over the world. Throughout history mice and rats have secretly found their way into people's luggage and travelled wherever they went. Sailors used to keep cats on ships to catch the mice and rats that came aboard in people's luggage!

Mice and rats live in the countryside as well as in towns and cities. They live mostly where people live.

House mice are well suited to living around people, in houses or barns. A lot of people think of them as **pests**.

Wild spiny mice eat insects like locusts.

Choosing your pet

When you have decided that mice or rats are the right pets for you, you will need to find them. Always get your pets from a good **breeder.** Never buy animals that have been caught from the wild.

When you are choosing your mouse or rat you should make sure it is healthy. It should be clean with bright eyes and be active and alert. It should have neat teeth and claws, a healthy tail and no skin problems. Watch the breeder handle the animal to make sure it is happy with people.

Choose a rat that is clean and healthy.

Mouse and rat habitats

Wild mice live in all sorts of **habitats**. Field mice live in fields and meadows. Wood mice live on the edges of woodland. Wild house mice are quite at home in people's houses and barns.

Wild rats live mostly where people live. Black rats like to nest in barns and lofts. Brown rats prefer to live in darker places, like holes under buildings. They also live on riverbanks and are very good swimmers.

Black rats are good climbers.

Your pet's cage must give it all the things it would need in the wild. Rats and mice need to be kept inside so they can stay warm.

Pet rats and mice need exercise. Their cage should have plenty of space for them to run about. The cage will need a floor covering as well. Soft hay is a good bedding material for mice and rats. You can also buy soft white paper bedding from pet shops.

The best cages are made from hard plastic or metal with metal bars.

Mouse and rat anatomy

Mice and rats have the same basic **anatomy**, although rats are larger than mice. They both have oval bodies, short legs, small feet with sharp claws, a long tail, pointed nose, and large ears.

Rats' tails are bald and sometimes have **scales**. Mice have tails that are smoother and covered in short fur. Pet mice and rats have the same anatomy as their wild relatives.

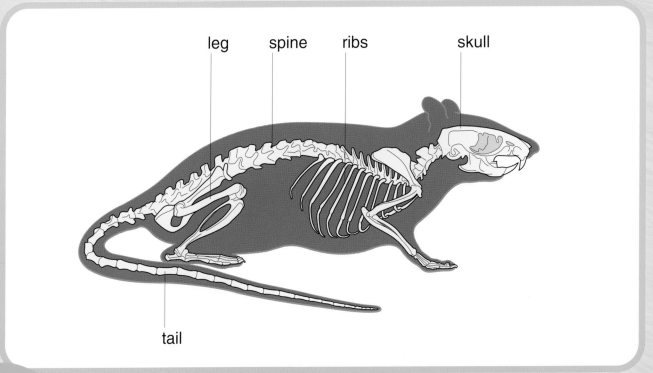

leg   spine   ribs   skull

tail

This drawing shows the skeleton of a rat.

Handling

Never pick up your pet by the tail. It is very delicate and can break or even come off.

Rats and mice are **rodents**. Rodents have teeth that never stop growing.

Wild rodents wear their teeth down by **gnawing** tough plants and nuts. Your pet must have a gnawing block to stop its teeth getting too long.

Always use both hands to hold your pet securely.

Senses

Mice and rats have very sensitive senses. They mostly use smell and hearing. They use their senses to avoid **predators** and to find food.

Mice and rats can only see well close up. Their eyes are better at seeing in low light. This is because they are most active at night. They also use their whiskers and **sensor hairs** to find their way around.

Mice and rats can hear much higher sounds than humans can.

Pet mice and rats use the same senses as their wild relatives. Hearing is very important for **communication** and sensing danger. Mice and rats have quite large ears to catch sounds.

Mazes

Rats can be taught to find their way in mazes. They use their whiskers and sensor hairs as well as their poor eyesight to find their way.

Smell is very important for finding food and identifying 'friends'. Mice use **scent glands** to mark their **territory**. They can be smelly animals, so they need their cages cleaned at least once a week.

Mice use all their senses to get around.

Movement

Rats and mice use their muscles to move. They are great climbers and run very fast. They use their tails for balance and to hang on to things. Harvest mice have **prehensile** tails that they use to climb grass stalks and to balance.

Speed

Rats can run at about 9 km per hour and jump about a metre! Mice run in short darting spurts of speed, and then stop still and check for danger.

Brown rats are very good swimmers.

Rats and mice need plenty of exercise and enjoy playing with all sorts of toys.

Exploring!

Pet mice and rats also use their short legs, powerful bodies, and tails to move and climb. Rats enjoy being let out of their cage to explore your house. This is good exercise and keeps them happy, but make sure they can't escape!

If your rats like being carried they may be happy to ride on your shoulder. They use their tail for balance and their claws to cling on when they climb down your arm.

What do mice and rats eat?

Wild mice and rats have **adapted** to eat many different foods. They mostly eat cereals and seeds. They will also eat nuts, berries, and roots. Field and harvest mice also eat small insects and worms.

A lot of wild rats and house mice have adapted to live near humans. They eat our food supplies, searching through rubbish and even our cupboards!

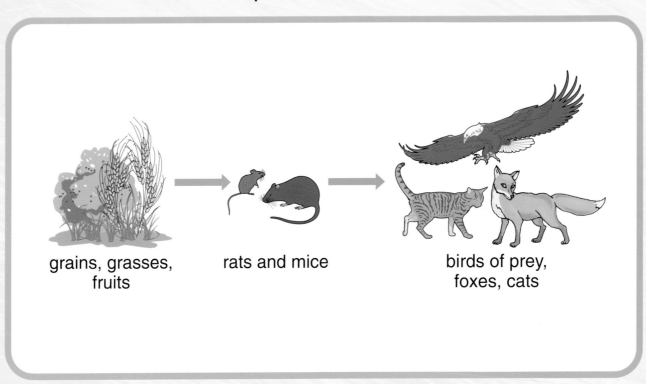

| grains, grasses, fruits | rats and mice | birds of prey, foxes, cats |

Mice and rats fit into a **food chain** like this.

You can buy special pet rat or mouse foods from pet shops. These include cereals, seed mixes, and special pellets.

Drinking
Your pet should always have a fresh supply of clean water. A water dropper bottle is the best way to give water.

Mice and rats also like to eat fresh vegetables. Plants that are good include dandelion leaves and grass. Small amounts of vegetables and fruit are also good – try carrots, cucumber, apples, and grapes.

Pet rats enjoy all sorts of food, just like their wild **relatives**.

Foraging and playing

Wild mice and rats are very active. They spend most of their time searching for food and staying alert for danger.

In the countryside they search out plants, seeds, and nuts to eat, and they hunt for small insects and worms.

Playing

*Young rats and mice play a lot. This helps them to **bond** with their family. It also develops their muscles for when they are ready to leave the nest.*

Harvest mice eat wheat that has been planted in a farmer's field.

Toys will help keep your pet fit and healthy.

Pet mice and rats cannot **forage** for their food. But you can make life more interesting for them. Scatter some of their food about their cage so they have to search to find it. This is like their natural wild behaviour.

Fun and games

You can buy toys like tunnels, ladders, and poles for your pet mice and rats. Be careful with wheels. They are not really suitable for rats as they can catch their tails in them.

Do mice and rats live in groups?

Wild rats need company. In the wild, they often live in big groups called **colonies**. Each rat has its special place in the group. **Dominant** rats are the boss rats. Dominant rats are usually the biggest as they get the most food.

Wild mice also live in groups. There is usually one male and several females with their babies. The colony has a **territory** where they live and eat.

This colony of black rats are all feeding together.

Like wild mice, pet mice are **sociable** animals. They are unhappy on their own. You should keep several male or female mice together. But don't mix them or they will **breed**!

Pet rats also like company. Two females together or two males is best, from the same family if possible. If you really can't keep more than one, don't worry. Your rat will like to spend a lot of time with you instead.

Mice like to play together.

If your pets haven't grown up together, watch them carefully to make sure they get on.

Sleeping

Wild rats and mice all need sleep. They are usually **nocturnal** animals, which means they are most active at night. They sleep during the day.

Rats make nests in their burrows. This is where they sleep and rest and give birth to their young. Mice also make nests in safe, cosy places.

Hibernation
Dormice hibernate during winter. This means they go into a very deep sleep to save energy.

Harvest mice build ball-shaped nests made of grass stalks, often in a field.

Unlike their wild relatives, most pet mice and rats have **adapted** to being awake during daylight. They are awake for some of the day, so you can feed them and keep them company. But they still have nocturnal **instincts**, so they need to be able to rest during the day.

Nests

Rats and mice need a nest box in their cage where is it cosy and dark. They will sleep and hide there.

Mice like to stay nice and warm when they are sleeping.

Life cycle of mice and rats

Mice and rats live for different lengths of time. Field and house mice only live for about 1 to 2 years. Brown rats can live for 3 years or more.

Mice and rats give birth to naked, blind babies. Male mice and rats are called bucks and females are called does. The babies are called kittens. Wild harvest and wood mice can have 3 or 4 **litters** of babies a year. Black rats can have about 5 litters.

A wild rat with her litter of kittens.

Mice usually have around 10 babies in a litter.

Pet mice live for between 2 and 3 years. Pet rats live for a bit longer, from 3 to 4 years.

Both mice and rats can have a lot of babies. A pair of rats can have up to 100 babies a year! You should always keep male and female rats and mice separately if you don't want them to **breed**.

Common problems

In the wild, rats and mice are often eaten by **predators.** They are also killed by people in cities and the countryside to keep their numbers under control.

Dormice are an **endangered species**. They live in woods and hedgerows. A lot of this **habitat** is being cut down, so the dormice have nowhere to live. But most mice and rats are not in danger.

The common dormouse is an endangered species.

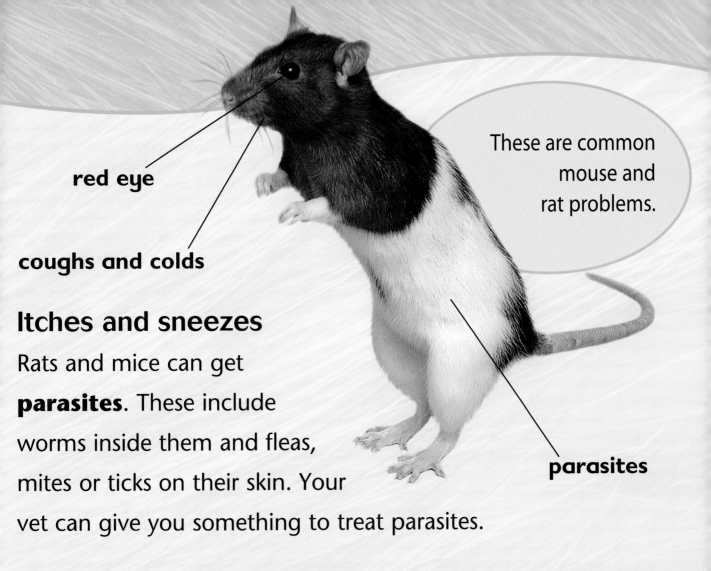

red eye

coughs and colds

These are common mouse and rat problems.

parasites

Itches and sneezes

Rats and mice can get **parasites**. These include worms inside them and fleas, mites or ticks on their skin. Your vet can give you something to treat parasites.

Rats can get red eye, which is an eye infection. Get your vet to treat this immediately.

Rats and mice can also get coughs and colds. These can be serious, so always check with your vet.

Now you know more about why rats and mice behave the way they do, you can look forward to a rewarding future with your pets.

Find out for yourself

A good owner will always want to learn more about keeping pet mice and rats. To find out more information about mice and rats, you can look in other books and on the Internet.

Books to read
Fancy Rats (A Complete Pet Owner's Manual) G. Bulla, Barron's Educational series, 2000
My Pet: Rats & Mice Honor Head, Jane Burton, Raintree, 2000

Using the Internet
Explore the Internet to find out about rats and mice. Websites can change, so if one of the links below no longer works, don't worry. Use a search engine, such as or *www.internet4kids.com* or *www.yahooligans.com* You could try searching using the key words 'mice', 'rats', and 'pets'.

Websites
This site contains a directory of all the mouse clubs in the UK: *http://www.miceandrats.com/other.htm*

This website has lots of information about looking after mice and rats: *http://www.rspca.org.uk*

Disclaimer
All the Internet addresses (URLs) given in this book were valid at the time of going to press. However, due to the dynamic nature of the Internet, some addresses may have changed, or sites may have ceased to exist since publication. While the author and publishers regret any inconvenience this may cause readers, no responsibility for any such changes can be accepted by either the author or the publishers.

Glossary

adapt become used to living in certain conditions

albino having no colour in skin or fur, with white fur and pink eyes

anatomy how the body is made

bond make friends with

breed when two animals mate and have babies

breeder someone who raises animals

colonies large groups of animals living together

communication making youself understood

domesticated living as pets instead of in the wild

dominant the strongest, most powerful animal in the group

endangered in danger of dying out or being killed

forage to search for plants and foods to eat

food chain the links between different animals that feed on each other and on plants

gnawing chewing, biting, or nibbling at something

habitat where an animal or plant lives

instincts natural behaviour that an animal is born with

litter babies that are born to the same mother at the same time

nocturnal awake at night

pests animals that breed in large numbers and cause damage

parasites tiny animals that live in or on another animal and feed off it

predator animal that hunts and eats other animals

prehensile can be used like another claw to hold on to things

rodents a group of small animals with teeth that keep growing all their lives

scales small hard patches of skin that fit together

scent glands parts of the body that produce a smelly substance

sensor hairs special hairs that the animal use to feel things

sociable likes company and living in groups

species type of similar animals that can have babies together

territory the area where an animal hunts and lives

Index